The Seasons

SPRING

Written by Stephanie Hedlund · Illustrated by Stephanie Bauer

magic Wagon

visit us at www.abdopublishing.com

Published by Magic Wagon, a division of the ABDO Group, PO Box 398166, Minneapolis, Minnesota 55439.
Copyright © 2014 by Abdo Consulting Group, Inc. International copyrights reserved in all countries. All rights
reserved. No part of this book may be reproduced in any form without written permission from the publisher.

Looking Glass Library™ is a trademark and logo of Magic Wagon.

Printed in the United States of America, North Mankato, Minnesota.
052013
012014
 This book contains at least 10% recycled materials.

Written by Stephanie Hedlund
Illustrated by Stephanie Bauer
Edited by Rochelle Baltzer
Cover and interior layout and design by Neil Klinepier

Library of Congress Cataloging-in-Publication Data

Hedlund, Stephanie F., 1977-
    Spring / by Stephanie Hedlund ; illustrated by Stephanie Bauer.
        pages cm. -- (The seasons)
    ISBN 978-1-61641-993-6
    1. Spring--Juvenile literature. I. Bauer, Stephanie, illustrator. II. Title.
    QB637.5.H44 2014
    508.2--dc23
                                2012049767

Contents

Spring

There are four seasons during the year.
Do you know what season is second?
That's right, it is spring!
Then comes summer, autumn, and winter.

4

winter

spring

summer

Autumn

Why?

Earth travels around the sun during the year.
When Earth is tilted so the sun is over the **equator**, it is spring.
The equator doesn't have spring, the **temperatures** stay the same for most of the year.

When?

The vernal equinox is March 21 or 22.
That means the days and nights are equal all over Earth.
This is the start of spring!

Earth's Axis

Night

Day

Equator

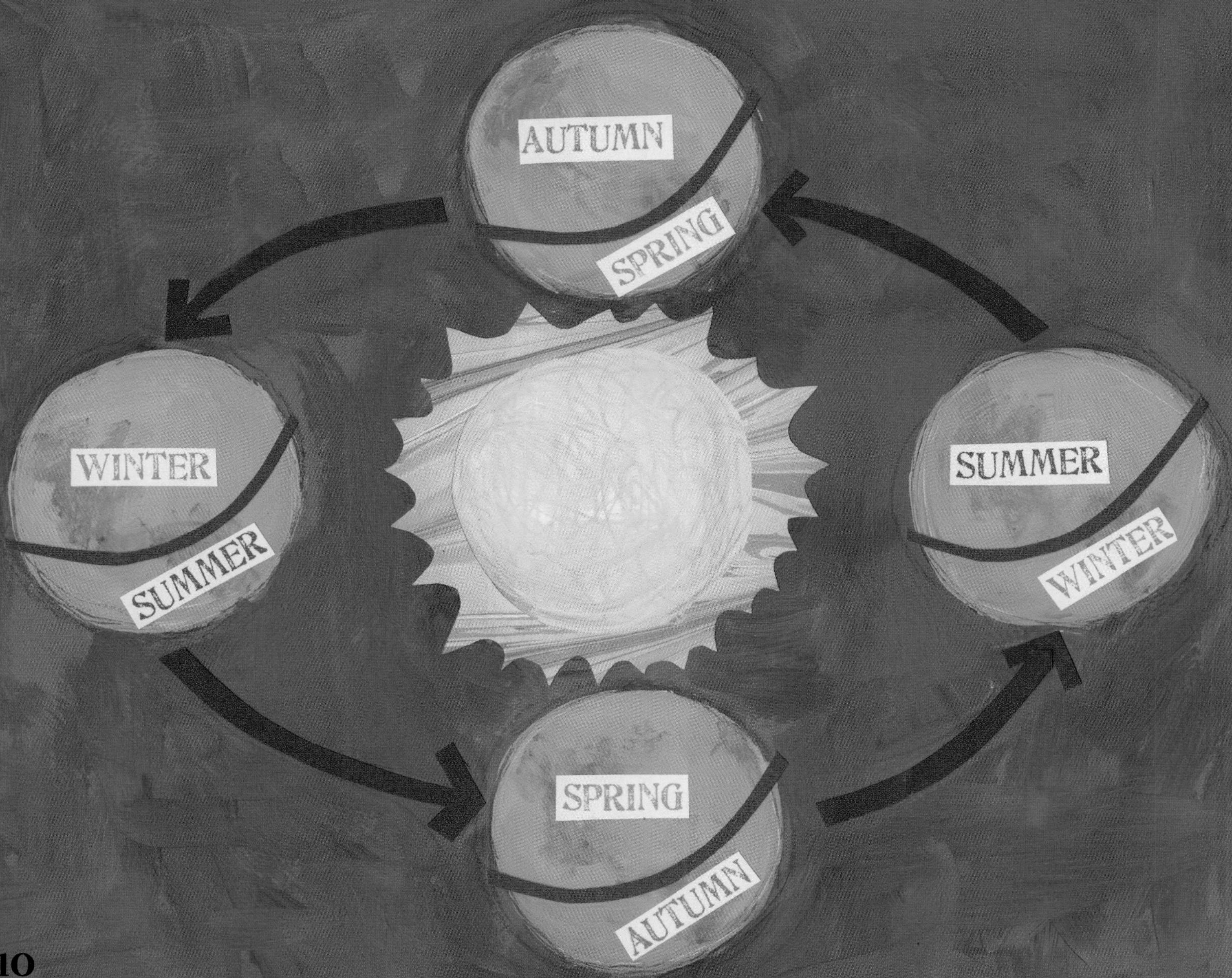
AUTUMN
SPRING
WINTER
SUMMER
SUMMER
WINTER
SPRING
AUTUMN

Spring lasts from March until June.
Unless you live below the **equator**!
Then spring is from September until December.

What's It Like Out?

In spring, the **temperatures** get warmer.
Snow and ice melts.

13

RAIN DARK wet
POUR
RAIN
RAIN DARK
THUNDER

lightning

It often rains in spring.
When warm and cold air meet in this season, storms can happen.
There may be **tornados**, thunderstorms, and flooding in spring.

What Do They Do?

In spring, plants begin to grow.
Many trees get buds.
Flowers, such as tulips, will bloom.

The animals come out of **hibernation**.
They wake up to find food.
Others return from warmer places.
They **migrate** to cooler places for the summer.

People spend more time outdoors.
They garden, take walks, and have fun.
Soon, it will be summer!
Do you know what will happen then?

Seasons

January	February	March	April	May	June
Winter	Winter	Winter Spring	Spring	Spring	Spring Summer

Spring Activities

Plant a Garden

Go Biking

Color Easter Eggs

Splash in Puddles

Go for a Walk

Make a Mud Pie

Make a May Day Basket

Web Sites

To learn more about the seasons, visit ABDO Group online. Web sites about the seasons are featured on our Book Links page. These links are routinely monitored and updated to provide the most current information available.

www.abdopublishing.com

Glossary

equator - an imaginary circle around the middle of Earth. It splits Earth into two equal parts.

hibernate - to sleep or rest during the winter months.

migrate - to move from one place to another to find food or have babies.

temperature - (TEHM-puhr-chur) the measured level of hot or cold.

tornado - a strong wind with a funnel-shaped cloud. A tornado moves in a narrow path.

vernal equinox - (VER-nahl EE-kwuh-nahks) the day in March when day and night are each 12 hours.

Index